AWE
and other words like
WOW

AWE

and other words like

WOW

POEMS

KAT GEORGES

THREE ROOMS PRESS

NEW YORK CITY

ISBN 978-1-953103-41-3 (trade paper original)
Library of Congress Control Number: 2023935369

TRP-108

Publication Date: September 26, 2023
First edition

BISAC Coding:
POE024000 Poetry / Women Authors
POE023060 Poetry / Subjects & Themes / Political & Protest
POE023070 Poetry / Subjects & Themes / War
POE023020 Poetry / Subjects & Themes / Love & Erotics
POE004010 Poetry / American / General

COVER ART AND DESIGN:
Susan Shup: www.shupshop.com

BOOK DESIGN:
KG Design International: www.katgeorges.com

DISTRIBUTED IN THE U.S. AND INTERNATIONALLY BY:
Publishers Group West: www.pgw.com

Three Rooms Press | New York, NY
www.threeroomspress.com | info@threeroomspress.com

for peace

staring
at the wall

        the wonder of it
              all

CONTENTS

AWE
and other words like
WOW

AWE

for Patti Abrecht

A child laughs
and so it begins.
A day. A glow.
A fortune in joy.

Trees embrace your
eyes with their magic.
Beneath the ground
roots talk to your toes.

This is not a rainbow day
or a saturated sunset,
simply the splendor:
A breath. An answer.

On days like this
the human voice
cracks the air
and each voice, each
word—even the most
mundane—sparkles
because it is full of
life.

Life, that game of who
can breathe the longest.
Life, that sudden merging
of infinitesimal with infinite,
a jigsaw puzzle which,
for a time, sits on display
with no missing pieces

till the dog begins to
sneak a few away.

Sky blue, blood red,
air the color of a
transparent rainbow.

Endless, and limited.

Life, where you get
a chance to soak
your shoes in a puddle,
or eat a slice of pizza,
or raise your voice at
a cloud and shout,
"Why? Why? Why?!"
one minute, then
marvel that clouds
and minutes even
exist.

This too is the marvel,
this too. And this. And
this.

Shout a big fat holy "Wow!"

Ain't that wild?
Ain't that cool?

Yes, and yes.
And yes.
Yes.

GOLDEN MOMENT

in the pink-orange predawn sky
tucked behind steel gray towers
the summer sun not yet risen
there, the mighty Hudson, blue green
at the confluence of sea and stream
lapping the concrete pillars of the piers
high under the silver moon's tidal force
at the path's edging gardens, see
thrusting pink coneflowers, delicate
pale hibiscus, fading lilac hydrangeas
and the green expanse of elms and
honey locusts, peppered with a few
spreading proud magnolias, and the
green expanse of Kentucky bluegrass
dotted with galloping squirrels and
mourning doves, always in pairs,
and strutting rock pigeons, their heads
a kaleidoscope of teal-grey-purple

my blue shoes mark time as I count steps and track goals

last night still haunts with its memories
today awaits, with its nemeses and practicalities

in this golden moment, in this
paradise of so much color
I keep moving

AIM FOR THE HEART

what if my heart beat
not like a drum
but a glockenspiel

each step a merry
ping!

in a single block
a melody forms

two blocks
a song pours out

each mile a symphony
of ringing bells

as glockenspiel
my heart emits
a cheery tinkle

penetrating
resonant

prelude and finale
beginning and end
start and completion

pulsing

PRACTICE MAKES PERFECT

for Ann DeJarnett

to create something as perfect
    in originality, form, shape, scent, and effect as
        a rose—velvet petaled hue of warrior blood
            a gardenia—gentle spiraled thunderous aroma
                a peony—radiant harlequined melodic bouquet

dance in shades, midnight moons, stare down suns and stars
    breathe fire, exhale glaciers, gently pet a porcupine
        fierce strokes, no erasures, ink or paint, destroy pencils
            envelop waterfalls, drink ideas of children and weeds
                skip through cities and old-growth forests,
                    quake earth, shake clouds
                        spell *gnihtyreve* backwards in your language,
                        read a kitten palm, laugh
                            practice love until you know its
                                secrets, forget, and do it again

        everything you create is
        as necessary as a lily
        you're not the gardener
            you are the garden
        perfection is your practice
            I hear your song in every wind
        but only if you sing . . .

REMEMBERING THE LIGHT

To remember only the dark shades
is to immerse wholly in a pool
that doesn't cleanse or even
feel like water.

To remember only the shadows
is to forget
the love—
the recognition that
love exists—in a daily meal
a smile, an elbow bump,
a phone call, a photo.

Passion pulling you out of bed
each day to find astringent strings
of moments.

Curiosity—
it's all the same,
nothing is the same.

Take the road trip
and compress it.

My daily route covers
500 square feet.

But I'm traveling
light-years every second.

Memories—flashes of places,
of canyon vistas, the sound
of church bells, the way my
mother laughs when she doesn't
really think it's funny.

Cookies from the nuns
across the street.

The other day, a total stranger
bought me croissants at the little bakery.
"Pay it forward, you know?" she says
with a laugh.

And the surprise of a kind word
daily—daily—in all the
noir—the hits keep coming
and I say—force yourself
to remember it all.

To see it all.

You only have to open
your eyes.

WHAT I KNOW

for Jenny Smith

I know there's a person
that holds me in their shoes
and arms the light of me
in their eyes

I know there's a bench
where I sit next to
a person with a velvet
razor in her purse

I know when I stand
and walk across the
room the window full
of light is on my side

It is a difficult birth
each day to place
the foot under the
table and the hand

under the chin
to ponder
consider
think
love

yet here I am
another day begun
another chance
to make the impossible
possible
to bring what is
now only darkness

into the light

if only for
one
earth-shattering
world-changing
moment

which is everything
and always was
and always will
be

ABANDON

be the abandon

be the crazy red-eyed man on the street
    telling every passerby, *"Gooooo hoooome!"*

be the young girl dancing in a park with butterflies

be the cosmonaut in a yellow space suit

be the man in the moon, be the woman

be the smile in war, picking plums off a low branch

be the New Yorker jaywalking in Beverly Hills

be the billionaire ex-wife who gives it all to charity

be the charity that gives it all to the people they are
    supposed to be helping

be the teen who helps a senior cross the street

be the soft raga of early morning, the wild sounds of night

be the distributor of pure, free joy

be, regardless, be

HANDS

I can't count raindrops or teardrops
only sheep as I pass them on the path
from vigilance to hallucination

drifting drifting drifting

stronghold of hypnosis
sanctum of temptation

embraced visions
flying without a plane
weightless body
hands like wingtips
gliding through walls
as if they were bubbles

freedom so plentiful
it doesn't have a name

where knots unravel
where sorrow has
no measure

INSTRUCTIONS FOR DROWNING
ON A CLOUDLESS DAY

imagine a darkening sky
thunder, torrential rain
your home floating
into the sea

open your medicine cabinet
determine the number of pills
you will need to stay alive
for another year

read every news article
about climate change and war
written in the past six months—
alternate with searching for
#humanity on social media

call your children or other relative
a generation younger than you
wait for return call

go to that hip new cocktail bar
"everyone" is talking about—alone

put your back to the window
and resolve to ignore the beauty
the world provides you daily
regardless of everything else

go ahead
I dare you

WHY I STILL WRITE ABOUT BEAUTY WHEN THE END OF THE WORLD IS ALMOST HERE

They say a mother's love is unconditional.

She will deflect bullets from her child to protect him or
lift a car three feet in the air to save her little girl.
She will scrimp and save to feed her child or
give him piano lessons or put her through college.

A mother will rescue her children, will run into a
burning building to toss a baby from the window
with her own back in flames. She will stand up
to a cop and say my son is a good boy, stand up
to a doctor and say save my daughter or else.
She will dive into the ocean to keep her child
from drowning. She will put the baby in the back
seat, make sure the baby sleeps on its back,
and always, always has her baby's back no
matter how old or troublesome he or she
becomes because we're talking about
mother's love, the ideal. The reality, of
course, is not always this perfection.

The other kind of mother changes the locks
to punish her children who stay out too late.
She drives her children into a lake in a car
with locked doors. The other kind of mother
simply does not care, ignores her children
with drink or drugs or lovers or mirrors.

My Child is not beautiful. She is Beauty. Very shy.

By day Her favorite game is hide-and-seek and
after dark She slips away leaving the starless
tick tock hollow flat. My Child is a torturer
who disappears and screams and stares.

I could be the other kind of mother.
But if I don't believe in ideals who will?

So I keep searching for Beauty and
every so often She hits me in the face
and says, "Here I am."

What more could any mother want?
Everything is different because of her.

ACUTE WITH PLEASURE

Remember when we turned up for the day new and acute
    with pleasure
Halloweens when we scooped out and roasted the
    jack-o-lantern seeds
hair done up with AquaNet and skirts so short we could not sit

Breakfasts of coffee, taco truck lunches, cilantro our favorite
    vegetable
dinner at happy hour—two dollar beers, all you can eat buffets
we didn't talk about dreams: we lived them between tears

We could have laid in that fallow field forever, until the money
    ran out, the car crashed,
the arguments started, the floors became hard to sleep on, the
    parties grew boring,
people grew older without growing, the fear grew: it was the age,
    it's always the age

Time does not make us who we are: we are formed moment by
    moment, but we lived
those days. Each series of coming moments so full of potency.
    Sometimes we still live
those days: in a saturated kiss, in an unexpected letter, in the
    heat of the dance

Between reports of friends getting sick, or moving, or worse—
    things you can't get used to —
things that make you feel the way a doe does leaping away from an
    oncoming fire until there's
nothing left to do but lie down in the soft meadow grass to quietly
    watch a butterfly disappear

ROSES

sit for a minute—stay

let us sing sad songs to each other
about the dreams of endless golden days
in pink cottages overlooking sandstone cliffs
dreams where we perched, you and I,
sipping iced green libations watching
boys become men mastering waves
kissed by gentle salty breezes
as sun breaks the marine layer
and roses begin to petal the sand
slender in their sunglasses, sneers
and neon-bright bikinis

let us brush each other's tears off
as our childhoods disappear, as our
days of glory wash away, as we become
the faded faces no one in our dreams can see

let us hold each other as we chant
the lengthening list of loss
let us help each other remember stories
to distinguish the gone ones
to flash them to flesh for a second
we are part of those stories
we must remember

so much pales in time
like shells on the beach
bleaching what once was distinct
to a blur

let us pledge, you and I, that
we will not be a blur
we will vibrate with passion
grateful, electric
each breath a part
of our limitless tale

STOP THIS BODY

what is your birthdate?

you see the hand   the head
   the eyes
move the eyes left to right
   read the fourth line

                   (please)
    identify   define commit

what is your birthdate?

count the spots   memory: sunburn
    skin never forgets
  more spots to come
save your money
        unpreventable

what is your birthdate?

measure   the heartbeat
  rate   pulse pattern
the heart is electric   expect a
        steady current
   not this

what is your birthdate?

   here come the pills
   get the plastic box ready
   M T   WTF   S S

what is your birthdate?

stop this body
   decay with

              memory
  regularity   slow age
no process   start with steel cut   oats
    no   sugar   salt
no   carbs   meat
          no   milk   alcohol
  consistency is   the key
boredom   is   not   as
  vital

what is your birthdate?

  the owner's manual
  is in the glove box

  drive

A WOMAN IS NOT A PEAR TREE

for example: no partridge required

for example: not born only to bear fruit

for example: when pruned, the preference is for
keratin treatment and two-process color,
preferably paid for on the barter system

for example: the savory offerings fall from these lips,
self-harvested

for example: the nectar of these flowers is sweet,
but please—no bees

for example: bare branches in winter? are you kidding?
it's twenty degrees out here!

for example: roots, but not so deep they anchor

for example: get those brandy bottles off my arms
darling, I'm dancing

for example: strong enough to carry the weak
for a while, sometimes

for example: a few nests, mostly songbirds

for example: that nighttime fragrance on a warm
spring evening? j'adore

for example: not bartlett, not anjou—not funny—
next!

for example: shoes

for example: this

SOMEWHERE IT IS

Somewhere it is dark
And war rains on a city

Somewhere a child
Celebrates his birthday
With a new soccer ball

Somewhere the stars
Make you feel as insignificant
As a worn out shoe

Somewhere the bartender
Sees you in the throng
Sets down a napkin
Looks you in the eye
Says, "What do you need?"

And you tell her so much
In the simple act of asking
For a beer

FLOWERS AS YELLOW AS SLICED LEMONS

She diced her days like tomatoes
Cubed moments cannot flow
Women crave control
Some sharpen knives for it
Lock portals, pull curtains
Hoard

You've heard of cat ladies
Open their doors to
The stench of decay
The shatter of reduction
Waste

What she was before—
There is always a before . . .

Those plum days when youth
Blossomed her cheeks

When a shy boy
Handed her flowers
The color of sliced lemons
Her hands so tender
Caressing them
Their scent

Torn from her arms
By a mother regretting
Her lost youth
Waste

We drive each other to madness
Women crave control
The temporal power
Releasing the sharp cut
The casual cruelty

We are rivers
If only we could
Remember

BOUNCE

Let's talk about renewal
Let's talk about the bounce

When you get that light light step
When you meet the street striding high
When negative negatives seem like a joke
And you wear problems like removable tattoos
Knowing they're only as real as they look
And looks can be deceiving

Renewal:
When you stare at the sky
And shout, "Why . . . not?"
Then get started drawing maps
Showing how you'll get from
Where you are now to
Where you are not now

You pack your suitcase with
People who get in your way
And throw it out the window

You are not on this earth
To be happy or sad or brilliant
You are here on this earth
To be you, in all your glorious
Flaws and fat in the wrong places
And a tooth or two that doesn't
Glimmer like a blank piece of paper
Your teeth have lived
You have lived

And you turn off the notifications
Of the mild achievements of others
Who'd make you so jealous
You'd hold your phone up to a mirror
And cry because you'll never look like any of them

You keep going when all you want to do
Is pack it in and play video games, watch movies
Or sleep sleep sleep

You keep going when the last thing
You want to do is shuffle off to your dull job
Cash your lousy paycheck
Stare at the walls and try to figure out
How to make the stack of bills smaller
Than the dollars left in your bank account

You don't want side hustle
You are full complete this-is-me hustle
You want to do the hustle
You want to dance
Past that past that everyone sinks into
And get your arms around a big fat
Dose of this life and say
    "Here I am—
    come and get me"

SELF-PORTRAIT

Lock on this face in a mirror.
Others will see what they want.
What I see varies depending on
  day of the week
  current mood
  most recent shower
  alcohol content of previous evening
  who died this week
  latest meal
  music being played
  music in my head
  fresh successes
  slap-happy pride
  momentary belief I am
  a failure at everything
  pending projects
  upcoming vacation
  amount of caffeine in system
  weather
  bank account balance
  hours spent crying
  hours spent laughing
  amount of grey showing in hair
  aches and pains
  number of cracks in mirror
  reality or something like it

Mirrors only reflect a moment

I prefer my self-portrait—
for years painted
in shades of black and grey
with highlights of red and
occasional yellow
something to edge
the shapeless swirl

Lately I'm adding more layers
colors in tones both muted and bold

Over my shoulder, a verdant valley
rolling hills splashed by sun from
an unseen source

After years of abstraction
a face is beginning to form

It looks like me

I think I like it

PREEMPTING THE SHY SINGULARITY

"By the year 2045 we will experience the greatest technological singularity in the history of mankind: the kind that could, in just a few years, overturn the institutes and pillars of society and completely change the way we view ourselves as human beings."
—Futurism

It will be morning. It will be a woman.
It will be tree leaves shaking in wind
as daylight fades the night.

She will face east, arms outstretched,
welcoming sun's first shy hello.

She will be life. She will be breath.
She will be heartbeat. She will be song.

It will be a pleasure to see her.

she is there to	be seen—she is	
not what she	seems to	eyes far away
our eyes of the	time, oh	to imagine
	the poetry of	her is
the poetry of women	the description in	
search of knowing	the words painted	etched
capturing a	moment a sky	
a woman in silhouette	but	

In this scene, this sketch, this is not a woman at all.
It is the project, the history, the metamorphosis, the ideal.

There was this woman.
There is this woman no more.

It is not her beauty you observe.
It is your beauty, your arms outstretched, your imagined being,
your muse, your force, your fraudulent ideas. It is in the after,
　　the agreed-to before.

This woman, this sun, this set, these leaves that shake in a place
that has no leaves and this is all there is and it is not.

To explain now, while this can still be explained.

To show the then what it is when the before is now
the machines not yet establishing what we will agree to see
in the unforeseeable soon-to-be.

The shift uncontrollable
irreversible.

The shy wave goodbye.

HUH

THIS CITY CATHEDRAL

here in this magnificent city
sunrises and sunsets are our stained glass windows
we live surrounded by massive rivers of holy water
the choir is a jazz band in a basement around the corner
our pews are subway benches and bus stops
our altar: bodegas where money turns into whatever you
    need
we measure communion in pizza joints by the slice
and sip wine at dive bar happy hours when it's cheap
and the rich are holy spirits we never see
and the saints—
the saints are everywhere—
cab drivers and bartenders
caretakers guiding the old around town
women pushing strollers that hold someone else's babies
neighbors helping tourists find their next adventure
the saints perform in tiny theaters with tiny audiences
they read poetry in bars and stay for bands that follow
they ride bicycles and deliver food in the snow
and dance down sidewalks and subway steps
and you can pretend that they have all disappeared
because of disease or crime or just because
someone decided that the world used to be different
or used to be better until
the liberals ruined it or conservatives ruined it
or the media or money
or the young or old ruined it
but I'm here to tell you
this city is a cathedral
and yes, I feel holy
right now

THE HOUSE WAS QUIET AND
THE WORLD VICIOUS

[INSIDE]

the dream continues
the mail arrives six days a week
the air conditioner cools the bed
made daily the occupants—a man
a woman—share nightly eat
together at noon coffee mornings
work from home discuss what
news drifts indoors insulate—
perfect as a fine souffle

[OUTSIDE]

the souffle falls, the city streets move
in individual tempos, each person a
moratorium freshly passed, separate and
anything but equal, temporary alliances
gathered at outdoor restaurant alcoves to
laugh and drink and drink listening to music
from a speaker self-supplied, creating their
own atmosphere, the chosen venue simply there
bend an elbow to their laughter and more laughter
heartless noise, a drink or phone in every hand, a
city of lost souls young, some in love, going and
coming to the park of the loudest, strongest, shy
acquiescence, and no one looks at the sky

a city of meandering, directionless, fog-eyed
a city in search of a leader to break, ready for
rules to crush until they crumble

YOU MIGHT COME HERE

in the little cafe around the corner
a woman sips mint tea and texts a secret lover
her husband orders her latte: skim milk, extra foam
a man laughs loudly at what he hears through his earbuds
a child scribbles in the latest book of a popular poet
his mom writes her now ex-boss; he just fired her on Twitter
a worker wipes the counter down, eyes an empty tip jar
the bathroom door flings open and a madman emerges
a few glance up—fear, concern—he leaves, running
you might come here, but I prefer the place next door
no phones allowed, no laptops, wi-fi, cash only, terrible coffee
the owner works hard and snarls until you get to know him
still there's a hum in the air—small talk and possibility—
meet you there when you get a chance

FROZEN SPARROW

and then just like that the world stopped—remember?
that evening after a full day of motion
we couldn't believe it—
climbed to the roof for a wider view
but it was—
everything was—
still—
the stillness

yes, you were there with me—remember?
the city landscape, the traffic lights turning
green yellow red for no reason
across the street the school without children
no plane trails, no helicopters
no bicycles, no pedestrians

even the rain
stopped
falling

you think I'm exaggerating? how could you forget?
the dried up fountain in the park
the boarded up windows

the only movement was sound
a siren's soprano coming closer

your face at the end
such calm inertia

the sculpted stasis
of goodbye

CUL-DE-SAC

Well-groomed houses line the street.
Manicured lawns, neatly-trimmed gardens.
The crows in the tree are a problem.
What they do to the cars, the noise, too many.
The trouble will be dealt with by the agency.
An issue like crows is bad for the neighborhood.
A blemish. Imagine if they pecked a child to death.
No. Don't imagine such horror. Not here.
It would never happen here.

PULL DOWN THY VANITY

for Matthew Hupert

> *"Pull down thy vanity, I say pull down.*
> *Learn of the green world what can be thy place*
> *In scaled invention or true artistry . . ."*
> —Ezra Pound, "Canto LXXXI"

I would write of forests, water, and stars
But this city sways, blocking the view
All that is permanent is not nature-made
Take plastic, take pyramids, take vanity
Pull down—

Embrace the green—ha!—I hug trees
Extol virtues of hot springs, prairies
rats, raccoons, deer, plovers, fireflies
My mind maps constellations for breakfast
Chomps on strata at lunch, I eat
Natural disasters as a bedtime snack
Don't tell me I don't respect nature
Pull down—

Shall I compare thee to a summer's day?
Summer days are full of smoke and piss
Seniors passing out from heat and humidity
Drunks in the street yelling *hoo-yah* all night
Days long as if lazy hazy will last forever instead
At most a string of three/four golden perfects
The rest is a sticky mess
Pull down—

Winter: Blues. Spring: Joy. Autumn: New York
And here we are again, back in the city
A swirl of a stew: both exotic and bland
Where heritage is erased or commodified
Where one friend finally outfoxes leukemia
And one shakes until the day's first whiskey
Where madmen control subway platforms
And rich men control everything else
Except little pockets of paradise where
We paint green worlds, scaled inventions
Not home, not a lifetime, not even a day
A stretch where the sun rises on tar beach
And sets as two homeless kids on pier 40
Figure out where to sleep for the night

BLUE TRAIN

it was the train
the start and stop
the movement
the rumble
the static
the bell
the doors
the push
the people
the people

it was the way
the woman
down the aisle
twirled her hair
then stealthily
touched her breast

it was the man
in the next seat
furiously clicking keys
on a small black phone

it was the child
in the father's lap
fat fingers playing
with his beard

it was four teenage boys
scowling and staring
and pointing and laughing
and acting tough and drunk

it was the woman
distracted by the book
then the rumble like a lullaby
coaxing eyes to shut down

it was the polished shoes
of the well-dressed man
pin-striped suit over necktie
over impeccably white collar
of a freshly-ironed shirt
eyes red

it was the woman next to
the stroller, cooing to a baby
that did not look like her

it was the two young girls
a few seats away from
an older set of watchful eyes
listening through one ear bud each
to a song that made them
giggle and blush

it was the fashionable woman
with the sneer on her face
exhausting a forced cough
near every stranger

it was the old man
with the cane in the seat
at the end of the car
slipping slipping slipping
into sleep and then more sleep

it was you
it was me
it was there
it was then
it was when
it was why

it is
no more

I WANT TO MARVEL AT THE UNIVERSE
BUT ALL I SEE ARE BRICKS

for Wendi Engelking

my sister on the west coast and her husband are going
to stay in a tent in Yosemite three days, two nights—
they're on the way now

they look forward to seeing Yosemite Falls
a massive 2,400 foot drop of snow runoff thundering
from a majestic rock cliff to the valley floor below

"It gives off so much energy," my sister says. "Pure energy,
and the smell of the pine trees and fresh air.
And the sound of the wind rushing through the forest."

she worries about mosquitoes and bears, apparently there are
more than ever now, she does not worry about the stars, she
looks forward to seeing millions

I check the online webcam view of Yosemite Falls—
six by six inch frame—truly majestic—
I get distracted by another video
of a building getting bombed
then turn off the computer and
look out onto Bleecker Street

I do not worry about bears or mosquitoes
and the stars will live on without me

outside my window I see brick, five stories high, interrupted by
windows reflecting the movement below—streams of people
it's spring in New York City

an orchestra of pedestrians chatter in the warm sun,
a radio broadcasts seventies soul,
a river of cars and taxis, a siren down Sixth, a man's laugh,
a woman's giggle, I swear I just heard
the sound of a young couple's first kiss

and the smell of the bakery below and cheap perfume
and auto fumes and little dogs
trotting beside two roommates from the apartment
around the corner, and there's an
energy here, the energy of people and more people
with all their loves and jealousies,
joys and griefs, dreams and nightmares, worried people
and people radiating
pure carefree bliss

people that bite like mosquitoes and rummage like bears,
but mostly stroll on by just
wandering the village as they do on Sundays—
a Sunday wander in the city of energy
people like pine trees, wind rushing through them

the sun will set soon and the night and its energy
will bustle forth, neon and a cadence of high heels and
high end sneakers, louder voices and intimate caresses,
the dinner crowd, the bar crowd, the would-be romances
coupling home to studios in Brooklyn or Chelsea,
the East Village, uptown and somewhere in the night,
a dwindling to near-silence punctuated by the occasional
roar of a taxi or a late-night lonely drunk

and my sister will see stars in Yosemite
and the stars will live on without me

NOW

LISTENING TO A STRANGER'S PLAYLIST ON SPOTIFY

For Mika Rautiainen

> *"Music is stronger than politics."* —*Jimi Hendrix*

People who study ancient civilizations
have never been able to agree
on why humans ever invented music

there are theories: google them
like music a poem is not here to provide
empirical fact

like music a poem a collection
emotions high notes low
notes rhythm and feeling

feeling

that deep feeling found
here in a stranger's
playlist on Spotify
and this stranger
renders his emotions
in a 40 song, 2 hour,
46 minute music stream

I track him down on Facebook
he's from Finland
well . . .

I send him a message
he'll probably never read
about how much I admire
the music he collected in
this playlist named after
one of my favorite songs
"Shimmy Shimmy Koko Bop"

like a poem, like music itself
the playlist is filled with highs and lows
jazz and reggae and sweet
acoustic guitar and ragas and
and soul and gospel and afrobeat
and bossa nova and pop
and electronic and sounds and
the whole list has me
feeling

feeling

that deep feeling found
in a secret space
where all the emotional torture
of the news reports and the
bank account and the cold
and the worry about the
future no longer exist

and I can see love again
not as an object lesson or
something to cling to but
as something that is

that my heart is full of

the "Shimmy Shimmy Koko Bop"
playlist of a stranger from Finland
is my hope and belief in the power
of airwaves and sound waves and
wavelengths that make the
status quo tremble in its presence

each song created from nothing
music meaning nothing
except as that tremble
like a poem
clearing a path
through the terror
and pain to a light
filled room of beauty

BLUSH

stare at the sky
dance in the sea
sift sun-warmed earth
through your fingers

give thanks
say a prayer

blush at each
new interaction
with nature

the way you would
if your family was justly
accused of hurting
a puppy

it isn't enough
anymore to say
"it wasn't my fault"
and point

fires roar
lakes empty
icebergs melt

children look for answers
and find a blank stare

pull out your phone
and share photos
of what used to be

RUN FOR THE HILLS

The sun is expanding.
The Earth's core stopped revolving.
A slab of ice the size of Greater London broke off from
    Antarctica.

As a child I dream I am in a house on fire.
Sit on the floor, write a note, draw pictures.
Laugh as the flames grew near enough to describe in detail.

Anyone else smell smoke?
Who do you call when you're the sole fire fighter?
I hear screams—are others paying attention?

In a world of sports fans, who cares?
As long as the power and wi-fi keep working.
As long as the home team occasionally wins.

MAGICAL THINKING

and the cloud turned from a dinosaur into
a widescreen tv . . .

and the crayon drawing of mommy
holding flowers became mommy holding
her iPhone, staring . . .

and the tender kiss turned
into a gateway to virus . . .

and the couple dancing, so in love,
transformed to the couple sitting, back
to back, talking to people who weren't
in the room . . .

and the poet became an influencer . . .

and the dream home became a
hotel room with a built-in office . . .

and the kid who all the girls ignored
changed into a man with a gun
in a classroom, in a shopping mall,
in a grocery store, in a gay nightclub,
at a parade, in his parent's dream
home-cum-hotel room with a built-in
office no one needs anymore . . .

MY GRANDMOTHER SAID

for Nanny

My New York grandmother said
Watch out for the dangerous moon.
Each crater marks a failed romance—
meaning pain, meaning heartache,
meaning all the things a young girl—
bent on magnificence—
must avoid.

My Texas grandmother said
I have seen the moon cycle on six continents,
studied the great teachers to understand its history,
shed tears when the first landing module touched down,
kept journals of my body and mind in relation to its wax
        and wane.
At 75 I find it most magical in its majestic ascent from
        the horizon of
an unencumbered ocean as I watch in silent awe from a
        small balcony,
reminded of my own rise and fall, a life of moments,
        some squandered,
many lived fully, and in that moon I see not sorrow or
        death, but the
continuance of all things we call life, the
        interconnectedness of all life,
the corporeal merging with air, for it is all one life, the
        animals, the birds,
and we, the novices of this vitality, naive in our
        importance, waging war
over minute infractions of an existence we know so
        little about.

Both grandmothers—long gone now.

Only the moon, cool in her brilliance, remains,
shedding light freely on those who need it most.

BIGGER THAN LIFE

after Michael McClure

"WE ARE DEEP INSIDE
dancing in the car roar,
dancing on the beaches in the car roar"
—Michael McClure, from "Stanzas Composed in Turmoil"

There is a time for joy and a time for sorrow
but now is a time for molecular emotion

Quick! Before the robots multiply—
we must embrace what we are
DEEP INSIDE

We are universes, expanding ever further
from the molten core we once all shared—
driven to drift and divide,
filling the spaces between us
with ever more junk,
distressing the trail of crumbs
we left behind us to remember
our way home

WE FORGOT THE WAY HOME

the way back to commonality—
the place before our divisions and revisions
that starting point of fullness
before the rumbling urge to stand apart
before the goal became exceptionalism
all we once were—together—before

WE FORGOT THE WAY HOME

we are driven to drift and divide
the goal is exceptionalism
our leaders are influencers
their goal is exceptionalism
our churches dissect us
their goal is exceptionalism

WE FORGOT THE WAY HOME

and deep inside we long to remember

The robots are coming!
The robots are coming!

They will succeed because
they will show us the way
to what they say is home

And we will follow them
laughing, snapping selfies,
exceptional—one and all—
even in the way we fall
headlong—together at last—
over the cliff

HELLO

for Kip Duff

hello—
I'm going crazy—wanna come?
                    in a while, not now—
    my socks are damaged
                    I am damaged
gotta fill these holes with something—
                    tenderly, tenderly   tender me fifty
    and I'll sing you a song
                            sing you to sleep
what's the golden rule? who wrote it?

    I am a diseased descendant of a diseased society—
            critique transaction-based decisions
(except mine) now where were we—
                        love? hello?

    I'll take two wallets and a snickers
                    two brewskis and an LED lightbulb
            two tutus from Tutu's Tutus Too
two of you anytime, babe—
                    hold that pose—sunlight on your hair so hot
                    answer me this, my dear brutalist
have you change for a quarter
(of what)
                                            pounder
                                            bag
                                            tank
                                            hour

hello—I'm going crazy—wanna come?
        take a ride in this shitstorm called life
    where cats act like they got all the answers—
but what do cats say about spiders the size of a child's hand
    parachuting up and down the east coast in summer

about time about face about to about you it's all about you
    dig the human tragedy unfolding on your phone
    while you check the map for the closest
                bar
                restaurant
                dry cleaners
                viral violin player

my heart is heavy—what do you recommend?—
        gluten free does nothing for me

I was weightless as a child, grateful to remember
              all these many years later

PIECES OF SUMMER

Something like a beach in California
but without its naivety. Something like a
concert in LA, steel-toed boots on forehead,
and the haunting ever after. Something like
a parade of tanks at Hollywood and Vine.
Something like a Black man beaten by four cops.
Something like the riots after and the friends who
fled LA and those who stayed. Something like
a San Francisco protest. Something like the cops
who blocked the street. Something like the bus
we rode to prison. Something like three days in—
and the haunting ever after. Something like
the hunger that love brings, but not the money.
Something like a year of Diet Coke and Fritos.
Something like a tow truck and your car, you
ignore the sense of loss. Something like cold
pizza for breakfast. Something like a Russian
poet: *Americans all complain, yet everyone has
a TV, a microwave, and a refrigerator.* Something like
the sorrow of knowing this. Something like pills
that make the sorrow end. Something like the
pills my boss hands me. Something like not
taking them. Something like a paradise that
isn't on a map. Something like the brutal
sun, you watch sandcastles wash away.
Something like the hand that pulls you back.
A piece of summer some call love. Something
like a beach in California but without its naivety.

MOTION ON THE NUMBER LINE

for James Georges

> *High school math textbook number line example:*
> *"Owing money is negative*
> *Having money is positive"*

And even here, in mathematics—
purest of all fields, home of brilliant minds
and puzzle solvers, theorems and proofs
requiring union of abstract thought with
the even-handed concrete form of numbers
numbers numbers—even here, in the interest
of captivating easily-distracted young minds
here the form is now interrupted by capital
as if the idea of less than zero is more easily
grasped by coins and currency, owed or owned
and by extension to imply that poverty itself
is negative, wealth is positive, and the rest is null, zero
as if the rich are to be admired, the poor despised
as if the emotive gains and losses of a heart
the surge of joy when love dances in to overfill it
the desperate claws of grief that scrape it
below empty are the real abstractions
as if what is most important
doesn't count

OVER AND DONE WITH

this week, I swear I'll stay away from
the hot news, the intrigue, the scandal, divide
I'll lay back and send out "positive vibes"
be grateful, spread love and kindness

reminds me of a woman I used to know
back in San Francisco—she swore that
by maintaining control of her mind
she'd overcome negative consequence

one day she went out to a nearby park,
found a patch of fresh poison oak,
took off her clothes and laid herself down
a look of pure bliss on her face

next day at work she rolled up her sleeves
and gloated about how no rash had appeared—
had to admit her new age outlook
might just be the real deal

until the next day when she didn't show up—
see, the poison kicked in after a day's delay—
covered in welts head to foot—everywhere—
left her laid out flat for a week

I figured she'd give up the ghost on recovery
but reality never struck her as very important
though she did steer clear of field tests
for the rest of our days together

those golden days in that gentle place
where ignoring the rest of the world for a while
was easy to do, between protests and heartaches
between concerts and friends and goodbyes

WHEN DOES THE DREAM COME TRUE

Raised on ads and formula
Cut out early for the other side
Still part of me believes some
Dreams that fortify society

Such as shiny new cars
Such as home ownership
Such as love, such as family

Such as early bird gets—
Such as hard work gets—
Such as a good girl gets—
Such as money gets—

Slam-a-damn-a-ding-dong
Winner! Winner! Winner!

Who put the bomp in the bomp bah bomp bah bomp?

All this life
All these lies

I'll take two electric toothbrushes for 400, Chuck.

Oh, look! Behind the box the pretty lady is in front of
It's . . . a new planet that hasn't been messed up yet!!

Ohmygod ohmygod ohmygod!!

Read the fine print:
You're on your own, champ

Alone at last!

Read the fine print:
Transportation not included

ROUGH PATCH ON A VERDANT LAWN

I ate wild blackberries as I watched the first moon landing,
picked earlier, north of Seattle. Such sweetness then.

As a teen, I had a silver bracelet honoring a prisoner of war.
I forgot the name. It might have been David.

I found a gold bracelet in the back of the closet, etched,
"To Kat, Friends always, David." I don't remember him.

My mother died three years ago. I study photos to
    remember. Her smile
when I was a child, the smoothness of her hand on my
    forehead.

My father studied the stars, then lost his mind. The full
    moon tonight.
His telescope. The sweetness. The war. Things I don't
    remember.

Things I do.

THE ARBORVITAE

in memory of Joseph Brodsky

darling you think it's love, it's just the tree of life
shivering in a breeze of the subway, shaken by
rivers of air, reaction to some, *"Calm down, Diane!"*
it's not all food and foreplay anymore, next month
you are expected back in the office, in person
according to the schedule, we will be as flexible
as possible, sure, the buildings are inverting as
the people return from their hovels and wonder
what will the holiday party be like this year?
participants of paycheck diplomacy, made soft by
months of running to the fridge between zooms,
how will they survive this onset of structure and
the interruptive meetings with the team and their
underlings? what will it take to turn out those
countless reports on time, to maintain a cheery
disposition when you have to stay late and miss
your ten-year-old's first recital but it's okay this
is America and we are here to get the job done
if you have any complaints, that's what twitter
is for—but please stay off during working hours

OOPS

OOPS

the earth is leaking
smog and bullshit pour out
the hole in the ozone
we know about plus
10,000 other holes
no one's noticed yet

the recent volcano
on the ocean floor that
almost took out Tonga?
that wasn't a volcano

that was Mother Earth
vomiting at the thought
of having to put up with humans
for another twelve or fifty or god forbid
hundred years

we're like lice in her hair
parasites on her body
we're a flea convention
bouncing around in planes
starting wars, hating each other

she doesn't care

as long as we pay the rent on time
and don't leave a mess in the kitchen

oops

time to get your things together
make alternate arrangements

just ask the rich—
they're always able to move fast
when the iron door begins to close

BLUE SKY

before I forget, let me tell you
what a blue sky is:
        a massage for your eyes
                a nudge, a mother's hug

                add a white seagull soaring
                        add a brilliant white puffy cloud
        add a distant sea horizon

                        add a cathedral
                                add a skyscraper
                add the Statue of Liberty

add those you love

                add trees and more trees
        add a monarch butterfly's orange and black
                bursting off this azure ceiling

                        add your dog, joyful, leaping toward it

                add your hands, rising over your head
        greeting this turquoise atmosphere like your best friend

lifting spirits of all beneath
its unvarnished cobalt existence

KABOOM!

our lives are hard to know, each time a flower bursts to bloom—
kaboom!—another drifts away, petals fade from gold to brown,
yellow to the ash of age, some dry and slowly disappear,
others turn to seed and scatter, a few are plucked from us in
 the dark
at sunrise we turn for our usual look and—*kaboom!*—
 nothing's there
but memory and perhaps a few leaves, like letters, from the days
we referred to them as perennials, certain to reappear, something
you could count on, better gardeners than us detailed them online—
kaboom!—unsubscribe—doesn't anyone tell the truth anymore?—
you, stuck now in your winter, surrounded by leafless trees,
 hard earth,
the calendar that ends long before the memory will—
 on the counter
count the empty vases, push them to the back of the cupboard
like summer clothes—no flashes of color left to fill this grey day

A WALK IN THE PARK

late fall lavender whorls
cling to stems as ready
to toss them off
as
daughter-in-laws are their
husband's aging mothers

rub the corolla
like a magic lantern

instead of a genie
you'll find a remnant
of summer's bliss

instead of three wishes
grant yourself a memory

not what you did
not what you ate
not who you were with

rather
remember one
exquisite moment
when your mind soared
reckless, singular

a memory that helps you
learn to remember

in a world of motion
we so easily forget
and are forgotten in

NOSE CANDY

Send me a dozen roses
A clove of garlic
Fresh-cut lavender
Camembert

Send me desert sage
A lock of baby hair
A wool coat just
Out of the rain

Send me the rain

Send me words
So full of life
I can smell them

The scent of love
In every soft petal

KILLER MOON

by the time
I found my camera
after seeing a killer moon
illuminate the space between
two city buildings—
engaging the dawn
with a mystical aurora
the way lovers embrace
without touching each other
a glance, the tilt of a head
silent acknowledgment,
the not quite fullness of it—
the organic form—casting
light before light is known
a shiver of pale gold
plating all in its presence
appearance of antiquity
unity of being part of
a larger whole—
by the time I found
my camera the moon
disappeared behind clouds
protecting its soul
as words describe
what it was

REMEMBER WHEN WE USED TO TALK ABOUT NATURE?

Yeah, there we were.
You and I in the forest.
Sniffing the air so clean.
Drifting into a nether-nether
world of pinecones and creeks.

Remember the way the wind
sounded when it sped
through the trees?

And the way the bark felt?
And how ancient things were?
We counted the rings
until we lost track . . .

We crossed a stream
balancing on slippery stones
polished for years by
mountain water and rain.

We knew the meaning of pure.

We climbed up a long way
to the top of the peak
just to see how far
we could see . . .

Miles.
Centuries.

And at night: the sky
all shine and twinkle.
We counted the stars
until we lost track.

Back in the city
we could still smell
the pines and
see the cleanness
long forgotten.

Not for long.

Not for long.

But to remember . . .

CROW

for Lisa Panepinto

> *Treat a crow badly it will remember for years, torment you at every opportunity. Treat a crow well it will reward you for years with gifts, unexpected kindness, spiritual guidance. Crows do not forget.*

dear crow, teacher, guide:
do not let me forget

give me the gift of endless memory
of all the love and kindness people
have shown me through the years,
don't let me forget the friends who
put up with my mistakes, gave me
their last match, fed me an apple
or egg when I was hungry, spoke
to me when they were unhappy
sharing with me that dark swirl
we are taught not to acknowledge

let me remember the daily gift
of sunrise's fresh start, nurturing
scent of a pine forest in spring,
the way a sandy beach cradles
the body on a summer afternoon
the embrace of our earth mother
the pale light of our phasing moon
the gentle unfolding of autumn
the blue freeze stillness of winter

crow, let me remember dates,
names, places, where I left the keys,
the daily medication, last night's dream

more than anything, dear crow,
let me remember the way home
and when it's time to go

THE FOOD OF LOVE

for Jason Georges

they say smoke
from this year's fires
contains trace elements
of things no human
should inhale including
lead and ammonia
bicarbonate of soda
tears of a forest
sorrow of stones
the remains of a
carved heart with
the initials T.I. + J.G.
blue sound of a
mountain breeze
no longer blowing
through the trees
and the moans
of a future generation
wondering what it was
to be lost in the woods
but for the breadcrumbs
you scattered on the trail
to find your way back home

DIG

SOCK IT TO ME

back when we were held together by thread
gathered at parks in Berkeley, Chicago, New York
patches sewn on jeans, fists needling the air
peace buttons stitched on jackets
knotted together by veins and umbilical cords
tye-dyed eyes looking over our shoulder
for the man who called us paranoid
even as he raised his camera, his baton,
his gun, we were us then and we were strong

sock it to me

spiders spin webs, and people spin yarns
and both are easily broken, by clubs at first
then time: hard time, a lifetime of thinking
the issues were all sewn up: the draft did end
schools did integrate, women gained the right
to leave their sewing basket behind and work
and drink and whisper "I am" ever louder

until the tables toppled and the fabric ripped
and the madmen who hold the strings of
our embroidered life grew bored or impotent
or maybe just old—old enough to feel it,
old enough to fear it, old enough to look
at grandsons and history books with their
names fading like penciled marginalia

our own echoed words sound like a curse
woven into a tapestry that now appears to be
pure decoration—a hem unraveling an era

sock it to me

no one says that anymore
let the unwinding begin

KNEAD THE BREAD

Knead the bread.
Not the rope.
No when know means know.

Shall I say peace is an azure sky, contrasting
Autumn's burnt orange leaves.

All that ugliness in the world
and yet this kiss of deep breath.

Shall I say war is . . .

I try not to talk about politics
because I can't do anything
about the state of the world.

A vote here. A vote there.
Prayers six nights a week.

Shall I say love is what will save us
or shall I just chant it during protests,
stow it in an overnight bag when
not in use.

Did you see the moon tonight on tv?
And outside, the helicopter's spotlight
keeps a city safe enough for sleep.

THIS IS AMERICA

We meet on the dance floor and boogie down
to the evening news and the latest trending
social media rumors between idle chatter
about which celebrity died today and
the weather, exchange notes on current
medical status, exercise regimen, plusses
and minuses of city living, latest books,
concerns about the future . . .

We try not to dwell too much on the future.
This is America, we live in the moment,
scrappy optimists with little sense of history.
We are bar crawlers, rock 'n' rollers, we are
Harley-Davidson and Peterbilt, we are DIY,
we let the rich figure out the five-year plans
and know we won't ever be rich, just scraping by
with our smart tvs, our smart phones, our
smart appliances, and all the mobile security
apps we can handle, keep our cars safe, our
homes safe, our bodies safe—well, two of three.

We don't talk about bodies much. This is
America, we live in a land that worships youth
and football, calls sex education grooming,
then destroys the futures of pregnant teens
by forcing children to have children, it's all love
and morality till the baby is born, after that
you are on your own. This is America—where
good health is not important we don't want
sick people in this country, and when a cure
can prevent severe illness and death, in America,

we say it must be bad for you, only idiots take
vaccines, and if you seriously think everyone dies,
we've got religion to prove you wrong.

We will dance our asses off, because this is America,
we don't do anything half-assed, but no-assed is
a different story. This is America and don't tell us
we're living a dream—we will wake up and force you
to understand reality is the dream. What we do is live
free and we've got the guns to prove it.

Any questions?

ENORMOUS

what does a sunflower sound like
pelted with missiles and shrapnel

listen from four thousand miles

sound in vision: look

    a widow's damp eyes
    empty vases on tables
    rooms with no walls

bored with this story
change channels

    a child disappears
    from a stroller
    in less time
    than it takes
    to scrape off
    a lottery ticket

check the numbers
curse that you've lost
the last thing you need

THE RISE AND FALL

for Ariel

> *"We're born naked and the rest is drag."* —RuPaul

humans have will
humans have choice

mothers scream at school board meetings
and queer books are banned

priests force themselves on young altar boys
still, after all these years

lawyers lie to promote their cause
politicians lie to promote whoever's paying them

and somewhere in a subway station
that now serves as a bomb shelter
two children embrace under a blanket
struggling to stay warm on hard concrete
as air raid sirens wail

I am a bird with wings that only know how to fly
a tree with leaves that seek the sun
an ocean rolling an ocean dying
an ocean not in control of its tides

rising
falling

rising
falling

THE WAR

you want to wake up
you want to say
"it was only a dream"
"this was the last one"
"the only one"
"a fluke"
"it will end soon"
"peace will reign"
"love trumps hate"

you want to imagine the history
of humanity highlights stories of
random acts of kindness
hand-holding, hugs, smiles
nations full of boundless joy

it does not

but somewhere, even in
the midst of all this madness
two men share a golden apple
girls skip rope on a city sidewalk
a young boy learns the alphabet

a woman gazes at her child
eyes full of unbridled love
coos to her, "one day, one day . . . "

OVER AND DONE WITH

revolutions start in the spring
and sometimes they succeed
and most times they at best
appear to succeed, with
the same old cronies
trading chairs but staying
in control

you read about the ones
that go to prison, clap hands
and say "justice has prevailed"
while the men behind the curtain
keep pulling the strings

easy to get caught up
in the futility of the con—
not just long but ongoing

that is how they win
them, they, those entities
that are not you or me

get caught up and
you start missing things
beauty, breakfast

get caught up and
you start believing sleep
is more attainable than
joy from a night of theater
a robin's call, a phone call
with a friend, the touch
of your lover

that is how they win

get caught up and all this—all of it—
may as well be over and done with

on the other hand—
before the days grow shorter—
what are you doing
tomorrow

MEN AND BITS OF PAPER

we watch the war on
twitter and television
gasp at the cruelty
pray our side wins
count the days

watch the buildings crumble
around the pregnant woman
with a face of disbelief within
a bloody abstract frame
count the refugees

watch the brave child
sing a stirring anthem

count the rapes
shudder at the brutality
missiles aimed at theaters
mines planted in radioactive soil
backyard graves dug by survivors

count the dead children

and finally it is all too much
we lose interest or at least
ability to pay attention

wish it all was over now

the way games end
the way movies end
the way the season
we binge watch
that which ends

why won't this end?
why won't this end?
why won't this end?
why won't this end?

PEACEFUL REVOLUTION

I wanted a peaceful revolution but
all I got was a peaceful easy feeling
and double the amount of email
demanding donations to prevent
an otherwise apocalyptic future

In desperation I deleted my email account
gave my computer, television, and phone to charity
and started to talk with people face to face

Now I sit in the little park on Sunday, Tuesday, and Friday
feed the birds and squirrels, talk to neighbors and children
construction workers and hard-working bicycle delivery men

When it rains, I walk for miles

I love to walk in the rain, each step
a baptism of ancient tears

in each puddle, reflection
of what could be

SEEDS OF VIOLENCE

watch the rain falling falling
what garden will it water

what seeds will germinate
what will grow

puzzles of history lie unsolved
who won what when

for clarity, see footnotes:
1) the face of a mother grasping a folded flag
2) a child in a factory unknitting the American dream
3) the teen trading tears for ammunition, mapping
directions to school

for clarity, see options:
the unvanquished, levering lightward

watch the rain falling falling
not all gardens are dying

we sprout unnoticed in
unheated rooms and vacant lots

ready to gather
in sanguine bouquet

our deep deep roots
blooms of dreams

too resilient to crush

WoW

THINKING ABOUT LOVE

When I think love, I don't think
about hearts and flowers and romance novels
full of princesses and pumpkin coaches
stars and tender kisses stolen on sweeping
castle staircases. Rapunzel letting
down her hair to meet the man again.
The glass slipper, the heartshaped box
of chocolates, the first dance, the
plastic frozen faces in the photos
on the wall, the woman in virginal
white, her partner in the tuxedo, the
extended family, standing tall,
their faces longing for the first champagne.

Break it out. Please.

When I think about love
I think this:

The absence.
The return.

To know love is to fill a glass
with water then hide it,
to spend days or months
without a sip, then, lips parched,
eyes dry, throat so tight you
cannot speak—then and only then—
to find the water and taste it,
drink it down, feel the sweet
joy of reuniting with something
you need so badly to stay alive.

When I think about love,
I know that I am the one
who has hidden the glass,
and that I am the one
who can find it—again and again—
sipping the liquid of life.

Making sure I remember
It is there.
It is mine.
It is what I need.

I HAVE WASTED

I have wasted days in lingerie
and nights in formal attire
tripping down memory lanes
that lead nowhere

I have wasted years in fear
of expectations and mice
disguised as authority figures

fear of saying the wrong thing
in casual conversation

fear of rejection and
fear of success

wasted nights disappearing
in liquor and drugs to have
something else to blame

I have wasted money
then again—not much—
what is money anyway but
something to waste
after the bills are paid

I have wasted hours worrying
about why I don't have enough
money to pay the bills

I could say I have wasted
time most of all
but those days of so-called waste
led me to you

your bright eyes
your tender heart

renewal in each kiss

I have wasted nothing

HALF A LIFE AGO

half a life ago
there was no you
and no me

fellow sparrow—
glance to passion
thought to creation

in our half life
we surge—defy gravity
shallow the deep

half a life ago
I did not know
love that ages
complex bitter enhanced

we are fortune
with a long half life
a-go-go mirrored ball
mesmeric lit dance floor
tango for two

half a life ago
worlds fell into place
planets aligned

the first kiss bloomed
to this

VISIONARY IMPULSES

Tell yourself that all of this is real
The light on the desk
The phone, the plant
The television in the other room
The smell of popcorn in the air
Overlaying a hint of this morning's perfume
Overlaying the scent of the bakery downstairs
The beautiful women in the clothing ads
The beautiful men at the gym
The weathered men delivering food
The young women full of worry
The young men strutting for attention
All of this, here and now

And yet you remember . . .

How real is a memory
Compared to a handful of ice?
The taste of salt on your tongue?
The voice of a friend, saying hello?

And yet you remember . . .

The past is a vision
Reality removed
The everything that led to here
The sum of all fear

OVER THE RAINBOW

took a trip over the rainbow
looking for a pot of gold
and found love instead
and a city where dreams
only come true for the
beautiful, trust-funded,
well-connected, and rich

but what's a dream really
fragment of a figment

I'll take love with
a roof and daily meals
the occasional postcard
from the world of mystics
and all the wonder
money can't buy

place my ruby slippers
on the curb with a
handwritten sign:
"free"

LIGHT

The brilliant way
You unleash light
Your eyes
Your radiance
You, the sun,
Compelling
Others to nurture,
Grow, even as
Your own sun
Sets within

Most of us
Too blind or
Too exuberant
To see the
Coming dark

IT HAD TO BE YOU

it had to be you and no other
standing alone, outshining the sun

count the steps to reach you
nearer, nearer still but never
there

how can distance keep dividing

the stability of your infinite half-life
you remain—forever—receding

I could kiss the stars more easily
touch the hem of all the saints
move war-mongers to abandon weapons
replace forests in the disheveled amazon

and still—there—you remain

blue mountain on a crisp horizon

catalyst of could-be

tell me how much further
reveal truth in equation
distance times hours divided by days
left

IN A TIME OF JOY

for Peter

In a time of joy
we run like children
careless, carefree on
parks and streets
the laugh, the dance
the need for nothing
bubbly as champagne
buoyant as the cork
unbound by deaths
of aged friends.

Life is gravity
in a time of joy
we dare reality
to catch us—
knowing it always
wins at the end—
but in a time of joy
we expand.

We are music
we are trees
we are history
rewritten without
conquerors, kings,
religion, wars, light
in dark corners
true as grief
bright as an
autumn moon
rising, setting
waning.

BLACK HOLE

sometimes love is
the misplaced key
the out of print book
the letter never mailed
the button on the floor
the coins in the couch
the Christmas tree on the curb

lost in the black hole
of the aging mind

still there, in need of
attention

dare to remember

I FOUND LOVE

I found love in a concrete stairwell once
and what I thought was love in an LA alley.

I found love in a magazine, a shower, and once,
under a table, after dessert.

I found love in a San Francisco nightclub, next to the bar,
listening to poetry on my knees, zipper down.

And in San Francisco, I found love in a storefront theater,
bed on a loft, stage for a kitchen, dead ass broke and happy.

I found love on the redeye to Chicago, once, swapping
stanzas from "The Four Quartets" as others slept
the flight attendant inexplicably bringing more vodka.

I found love in a San Francisco SRO hotel, pay by the week,
no discounts, no delays.

I found love in North Beach, wandering streets and bars, sipping
bitters for hiccups, reading, writing, nomad in the fog.

I found love in my parents eyes telling them I'd be moving
3,000 miles away, "We just want you to be happy."

I found love on Canal Street, newly arrived in NYC, standing still
listening to five conversations—each in a different language.

I found love after a New York blizzard, starving, trying to hawk
a trumpet at a pawnshop, just as three angels walked past
and dropped two fifties and a ten on the fresh-fallen snow.

I found New York poetry readings and I found love again, jamming
with Hydrogen Jukebox, nervous at Bowery Poetry Club, absorbed by
Cornelia Street Cafe: endless open mics, themed shows, wine and
words and wine and words and—oh yeah, I found love there.

I found love in three rooms writing, reading, making
books dance, listening to records, dancing in-between—
oh yeah, I found love there.

I found love with no money and love with some money,
but never found love of money leading to love or anything like it.

I found love in one person, a gift that makes me radiate love,
to share all I have found with anyone who has not found love
in a leaf, a notebook, a child's eyes, laughing.

So much pain everywhere.
Rivers of pain, gutters of pain.
And yet, in this breath,
I found love again.
In this breath,
reading these words,
I found love.
I found you.

WRONG

there is no right
there is no wrong

there is only love
and sometimes
a gun

a kiss
and sometimes
a lot of angry talk

a smile
and sometimes
tears in a mirror

a touch
and sometimes
a punch in the face

a warm memory
and sometimes
the horror

a stillness
and sometimes
a robin singing
its heart out
as you make
your way
along the
path

LUMINOSITY

let's drop the news for the night
drop the politics, the masks, the wars
the he said she saids
the shocking new polls

drop the disbelief that another rich one
got away with another bullshit crime

drop the stomach churning sense of futility
that the future once so bright is now dim

drop the need for spectacle as escape
drop the need to explain our malaise
drop the need to complain about
the electric bill, the phone bill
the credit card payment
the bank account of no return
the hunger

drop everything except you and me right here
just us for who knows how long

drop the need to mark time passing
here, in this eternal moment
drop all but our deep look into
the luminosity of each other

the searing glow that brought us together
the internal radiance that never fades
except through distance and the obstacles
we place between us, obscuring
memory of what light remains

TALK TO ME

Talk to me—gently,
the way you coo to a baby.
I need that softness today,
the sweet, slow dangle of diphthongs
that flutter like kisses off the tongue,
delicate ambrosial waves of words.

I don't need the three-beer har-har-har,
some business confab lingo,
and please—no news, no schmooze,
no medical discussions, no sports,
no regrets.

Just talk to me, quiet and bold,
introspective: the art of conversation,
a drift like tadpoles from lily to lily,
dwelling on metaphysics of possibility,
the meaning of breath,
the hilarity of each new day.

Talk to me. Touch me.
Meld with me in this
finite infinity.

NEXT TIME WE MEET

next time we meet
I'll be the white carnation
the cigarette in the left hand
the red scarf
the purple hat

call to me
I'll answer as agreed
with a whistle
a limerick
a hey-dee-ho-ha
a sneeze

you'll know it's me
by the way I drop
my handkerchief
my facade
my guard
my drawers

when you are certain
come to me
come with me
in me

don't worry
it's not a case of
mistaken identity

trust me
I'm
the
one

NEVER GIVE UP

sipping tea, late night
jazz on the radio
dim glow of a gone by

enter a melancholy
song—Coltrane ballad—
"Easy to Remember"

the music soothes
the slow accounting
of things I didn't do
relationships missed
chances never taken
places I'll never see

tonight comes down
like a heavy fog
lights bounce off
the way forward
no way to see what's
coming at you
the past a blur you
can't get back to

the song slides to
its sad sweet close
the semi-silence now
a heartbeat serenade

"be easy on yourself tonight"
I whisper and
"tomorrow . . . "

ACKNOWLEDGMENTS

"Awe" originally published in *LOVE LOVE Magazine* Issue 3, 2020-1022; also *Pocket LOVE LOVE*: 2019-2022); ed. by Lisa Marie Järlborn, Paris, France.

"I want to marvel at the universe but all I see are bricks" originally published in *NYC from the Inside,* ed. and with an introduction by George Wallace; 978-1421837178, Blue Light Press, August 2022.

"Preempting the Shy Singularity" originally published in *Arriving at a Shoreline,* 979-8985563313, Great Weather For Media, August 2022.

ABOUT KAT GEORGES

Internationally known poet and playwright, Kat Georges co-founded
San Francisco's Marilyn Monroe Memorial Theater in 1992, where
she served as co-artistic director for eight years. Her books include
the poetry collections *Awe and Other Words Like Wow, Our Lady of the
Hunger, Punk Rock Journal,* and *Slow Dance at 120 Beats Per Minute.* Her
work has appeared in journals worldwide, including *The Outlaw Bible
of American Poetry* (Thunder's Mouth Press), *Arriving at a Shoreline*
(Great Weather for Media), *From The Inside: NYC Through the Eyes of
Poets Who Live Here* (Blue Light Press), *The Verdict Is In* (also editor;
Manic D Press), *LOVE LOVE Magazine* (Paris), *Ladyland: Anthologie de
Littérature Féminine Américaine* (13E Note Editions), and many other
publications. Her nonfiction prose and essays have been published in
San Francisco Examiner, Orange County Register, La Habra Daily Express,
and more. She was born and raised in Southern California, where,
following her graduation from California State University, Fullerton,
she published *The Eye Magapaper,* an acclaimed music journal
covering the SoCal punk scene in the early 80s. She is co-founder
and co-director of Three Rooms Press. She lives in New York City.

RECENT AND FORTHCOMING BOOKS FROM THREE ROOMS PRESS

FICTION

Lucy Jane Bledsoe
No Stopping Us Now

Rishab Borah
The Door to Inferna

Meagan Brothers
Weird Girl and What's His Name

Christopher Chambers
Scavenger
Standalone

Ebele Chizea
Aquarian Dawn

Ron Dakron
Hello Devilfish!

Robert Duncan
Loudmouth

Michael T. Fournier
Hidden Wheel
Swing State

Aaron Hamburger
Nirvana Is Here

William Least Heat-Moon
Celestial Mechanics

Aimee Herman
Everything Grows

Kelly Ann Jacobson
Tink and Wendy
Robin and Her Misfits

Jethro K. Lieberman
Everything Is Jake

Eamon Loingsigh
Light of the Diddicoy
Exile on Bridge Street

John Marshall
The Greenfather

Alvin Orloff
Vulgarian Rhapsody

Micki Ravizee
Of Blood and Lightning

Aram Saroyan
Still Night in L.A.

Robert Silverberg
The Face of the Waters

Stephen Spotte
Animal Wrongs

Richard Vetere
The Writers Afterlife
Champagne and Cocaine

Jessamyn Violet
Secret Rules to Being a Rockstar

Julia Watts
Quiver
Needlework
Lovesick Blossoms

Gina Yates
Narcissus Nobody

MEMOIR & BIOGRAPHY

Nassrine Azimi and Michel Wasserman
Last Boat to Yokohama: The Life and Legacy of Beate Sirota Gordon

William S. Burroughs & Allen Ginsberg
Don't Hide the Madness:
William S. Burroughs in Conversation with Allen Ginsberg
edited by Steven Taylor

James Carr
BAD: The Autobiography of James Carr

Judy Gumbo
Yippie Girl: Exploits in Protest and Defeating the FBI

Judith Malina
Full Moon Stages: Personal Notes from 50 Years of The Living Theatre

Phil Marcade
Punk Avenue: Inside the New York City Underground, 1972–1982

Jillian Marshall
Japanthem: Counter-Cultural Experiences; Cross-Cultural Remixes

Alvin Orloff
Disasterama! Adventures in the Queer Underground 1977–1997

Nicca Ray
Ray by Ray: A Daughter's Take on the Legend of Nicholas Ray

Stephen Spotte
My Watery Self:
Memoirs of a Marine Scientist

PHOTOGRAPHY-MEMOIR

Mike Watt
On & Off Bass

SHORT STORY ANTHOLOGIES

SINGLE AUTHOR

Alien Archives: Stories
by Robert Silverberg

First-Person Singularities: Stories
by Robert Silverberg
with an introduction by John Scalzi

Tales from the Eternal Café: Stories
by Janet Hamill, with an introduction by Patti Smith

Time and Time Again:
Sixteen Trips in Time
by Robert Silverberg

The Unvarnished Gary Phillips:
A Mondo Pulp Collection
by Gary Phillips

Voyagers:
Twelve Journeys in Space and Time
by Robert Silverberg

MULTI-AUTHOR

Crime + Music: Twenty Stories of Music-Themed Noir
edited by Jim Fusilli

Dark City Lights: New York Stories
edited by Lawrence Block

The Faking of the President: Twenty Stories of White House Noir
edited by Peter Carlaftes

Florida Happens:
Bouchercon 2018 Anthology
edited by Greg Herren

Have a NYC I, II & III:
New York Short Stories;
edited by Peter Carlaftes
& Kat Georges

No Body, No Crime: Twenty-two Tales of Taylor Swift-Inspired Noir
edited by Alex Segura & Joe Clifford

Songs of My Selfie:
An Anthology of Millennial Stories
edited by Constance Renfrow

The Obama Inheritance:
15 Stories of Conspiracy Noir
edited by Gary Phillips

This Way to the End Times:
Classic and New Stories of the Apocalypse
edited by Robert Silverberg

MIXED MEDIA

John S. Paul
Sign Language: A Painter's Notebook
(photography, poetry and prose)

DADA

Maintenant: A Journal of Contemporary Dada Writing & Art (annual, since 2008)

HUMOR

Peter Carlaftes
A Year on Facebook

FILM & PLAYS

Israel Horovitz
My Old Lady: Complete Stage Play and Screenplay with an Essay on Adaptation

Peter Carlaftes
Triumph For Rent (3 Plays)
Teatrophy (3 More Plays)

Kat Georges
Three Somebodies: Plays about Notorious Dissidents

TRANSLATIONS

Thomas Bernhard
On Earth and in Hell
(poems of Thomas Bernhard with English translations by Peter Waugh)

Patrizia Gattaceca
Isula d'Anima / Soul Island

César Vallejo | Gerard Malanga
Malanga Chasing Vallejo
(selected poems of César Vallejo with English translations and additional notes by Gerard Malanga)

George Wallace
EOS: Abductor of Men
(selected poems in Greek & English)

ESSAYS

Richard Katrovas
Raising Girls in Bohemia:
Meditations of an American Father

Vanessa Baden Kelly
Far Away From Close to Home

Womentality: Thirteen Empowering Stories by Everyday Women Who Said Goodbye to the Workplace and Hello to Their Lives
edited by Erin Wildermuth

POETRY COLLECTIONS

Hala Alyan
Atrium

Peter Carlaftes
DrunkYard Dog
I Fold with the Hand I Was Dealt
Life in the Past Lane

Thomas Fucaloro
It Starts from the Belly and Blooms

Kat Georges
Our Lady of the Hunger
Awe and Other Words Like Wow

Robert Gibbons
Close to the Tree

Israel Horovitz
Heaven and Other Poems

David Lawton
Sharp Blue Stream

Jane LeCroy
Signature Play

Philip Meersman
This Is Belgian Chocolate

Jane Ormerod
Recreational Vehicles on Fire
Welcome to the Museum of Cattle

Lisa Panepinto
On This Borrowed Bike

George Wallace
Poppin' Johnny

Three Rooms Press | New York, NY | Current Catalog: www.threeroomspress.com
Three Rooms Press books are distributed by Publishers Group West: www.pgw.com

CPSIA information can be obtained
at www.ICGtesting.com
Printed in the USA
JSHW080934200723
45105JS00005B/5

9 781953 103413